A Robbie Reader

What's So Great About . . . ?

HELEN KELLER

Amie Jane Leavitt

Mitchell Lane
PUBLISHERS

P.O. Box 196
Hockessin, Delaware 19707
Visit us on the web: www.mitchelllane.com
Comments? email us: mitchelllane@mitchelllane.com

Mitchell Lane PUBLISHERS

Copyright © 2008 by Mitchell Lane Publishers. All rights reserved. No part of this book may be reproduced without written permission from the publisher. Printed and bound in the United States of America.

Printing   1   2   3   4   5   6   7   8   9

A Robbie Reader/What's So Great About . . . ?

Amelia Earhart	Anne Frank	Annie Oakley
Christopher Columbus	Daniel Boone	Davy Crockett
Elizabeth Blackwell	Ferdinand Magellan	Francis Scott Key
Galileo	George Washington Carver	Harriet Tubman
Helen Keller	Henry Hudson	Jacques Cartier
Johnny Appleseed	Paul Bunyan	Robert Fulton
Rosa Parks	Sam Houston	

Library of Congress Cataloging-in-Publication Data
Leavitt, Amie Jane.
   Helen Keller / by Amie Jane Leavitt.
      p. cm. — (A Robbie Reader. What's so great about . . . ?)
   Includes bibliographical references and index.
   ISBN 978-1-58415-583-6 (lib. bdg.)
   1. Keller, Helen, 1880–1968—Juvenile literature. 2. Deafblind women—United States—Biography—Juvenile literature. I. Title.
HV1624.K4L393 2008
362.4'1092—dc22
[B]
                              2007000823

ABOUT THE AUTHOR: Amie Jane Leavitt has written dozens of books for kids, has contributed to online and print media, and has worked as a consultant, writer, and editor for numerous educational publishing and assessment companies. A Brigham Young University graduate, Ms. Leavitt is a former teacher who has taught all subjects and grade levels. She enjoys gathering exciting tales for her writing and photographing beautiful scenery as she travels. Ms. Leavitt particularly enjoyed writing this book on Helen Keller. It confirms her belief in the determination of the human spirit. Regardless of the size or difficulty of our obstacles, we can all live lives filled with meaning and purpose.

PHOTO CREDITS: Cover, pp. 1, 3, 4, 15, 16, 19, 20, 23, 24—Library of Congress; pp. 7, 8, 11, 12, 22, 26, 27—Courtesy of the American Foundation for the Blind, Helen Keller Archives.

                                             PPC

TABLE OF CONTENTS

Words in **bold** type can be found in the glossary.

Helen Keller (left) and Anne Sullivan in 1879. In 1902, Helen wrote: "The most important day I remember in all my life is the one which my teacher, Anne Mansfield Sullivan, came to me. I am filled with wonder when I consider the [great differences] between the two lives which it connects. It was the third of March, 1887, three months before I was seven years old."

A Teacher Comes

Helen could tell that something important was going to happen. Her mother had dressed her in her nice clothes. The house was ready for company. Soon, Helen felt the **vibrations** (vy-BRAY-shuns) of the horses as they pulled the wagon up the lane. Who was coming to visit?

Seven-year-old Helen thought it was just a regular March day. Later, she realized it was the most important day of her life. On this day, her teacher, Anne Sullivan (SUH-lih-vun), came to live with them. Helen could not see or hear. Anne would teach her how to talk and hear with her hands.

At first, Helen did not like Anne. She thought she was mean. Anne made Helen behave. She made her be polite and not kick and scream when she didn't get her way.

Anne Sullivan had been blind for a while as a child. Her father had left her in a poor house after her mother died. Some people wanted to help Anne. They paid for surgery on her eyes. This helped her to see again.

Anne knew how Helen felt to be blind. She understood what it was like to live in a dark world.

Anne worked every day with Helen. She moved her fingers in Helen's hand to spell words using a finger alphabet. Helen thought it was just a game. She didn't know that everything had a name.

One day, Helen and Anne were in the yard. Anne let the water from the pump run over Helen's hand. Helen loved the feeling of water. Anne spelled the word *water* into her hand. She did it over and over again. Finally, Helen understood. The movements in her hand told her the name of this cool liquid. She smiled and clapped.

Helen often talked about that special day at the well when she learned the word *water* and discovered the "mystery of language." She said: "That living word awakened my soul, gave it light, hope, joy, set it free!"

As they walked back to the house, Anne taught Helen the names of flowers and plants. Then Helen pointed to Anne and made gestures with her hand. Helen wanted to know who Anne was. Anne spelled *teacher* in her hand. And that's what Helen called Anne for the rest of her life.

Helen at age six. She was upset because she had no way to talk with others. She later wrote about her childhood: "The desire to express myself grew. The few signs I used became less and less adequate [AA-duh-kwit]. . . . I generally broke down in tears."

A Bright and Happy Child

Helen Adams Keller was born on June 27, 1880, in Tuscumbia, Alabama. Her father, Arthur H. Keller, was a captain for the **Confederate** (kun-FEH-der-et) Army during the Civil War. Her mother was Kate Adams. Helen was their first child.

Helen was a happy baby. She was excited to learn new things. She was always trying to copy what other people did. She had bright eyes that shone with happiness when she smiled. At the age of six months, she was talking. Her favorite word was *water*. Helen was walking around the house on her first birthday.

One day, everything changed for Helen. At only 19 months old, she became very ill.

She had a high fever. She tossed and turned in her bed because of the pain. The doctor was afraid that she would die. Her parents were frightened and cried a lot. They didn't want their precious little girl to leave them.

Suddenly, Helen's fever broke, and she started to recover. Her parents were amazed at this miracle. But soon they discovered that something was wrong. Little Helen wasn't quite the same anymore.

One night, Helen's mother was giving her a bath. Kate noticed that Helen didn't blink when she washed her face with the towel. She moved her hands past Helen's eyes again. Still nothing. Kate was afraid something was wrong with Helen's eyes, but she didn't want to believe it.

Later, Mr. and Mrs. Keller noticed that Helen never responded to noises. A loud bell was rung at dinnertime to call people in from the farm. Helen never jumped or even moved when the bell rang. Her parents stood behind

Helen's mother, Kate Adams Keller, was relieved when her daughter survived her fever. She later found out how the fever had affected Helen's body.

her and yelled her name. She didn't turn around. She just kept playing with her dolls.

Mr. and Mrs. Keller finally realized the truth. Their little girl had survived her illness, but it had left her both **deaf** and blind.

11

Helen, Anne, and Alexander Graham Bell are using three different types of communication. Anne is speaking to Dr. Bell. Helen is listening to what Anne is saying by feeling the movements of her lips. She is also using the manual alphabet in Dr. Bell's hand.

A Dark and Silent World

Few people are both deaf and blind. For them, the world is silent and dark. They cannot hear birds chirping in the trees. They cannot hear the sound of their parents' voices. They cannot see the faces of family and friends. They cannot see a blue sky, the sparkling snow, or the bright colors of flowers.

Communicating (kuh-MYOO-nih-kay-ting) with others is also a challenge. People who cannot see or hear do not know when someone is talking to them. It must have been very hard for Helen. The child had known sights and sounds at one time, but after her fever, she awoke to a dark and quiet world.

Helen would sometimes behave badly. She didn't want to be a problem child. She was just **frustrated** (FRUS-tray-ted). She could not tell her parents what she wanted. She did not know when they wanted her to do things. When she would get angry, she would lie on the floor and kick and scream. What were her parents to do? They must have been just as frustrated as Helen was.

One day, Helen's parents decided to take her on a trip. They went to Baltimore to visit a doctor. Maybe he could fix Helen's eyesight, they thought. The doctor could not, but he told them to talk to Alexander Graham Bell, the famous inventor of the telephone. Bell's mother and wife were deaf, and he did many things to help deaf people. Maybe he would have an idea to help Helen.

Alexander Graham Bell and Helen became friends right away. He could understand her hand **gestures** (JES-churs). He was very kind to her. He told Mr. and Mrs. Keller about Michael Anagnos (ah-NAHG-nohs), the principal of the Perkins School for the Blind.

When she was older, Helen learned how to horseback ride. How could she ride a horse when she couldn't see? She said: "I just hold on to the horse and let him run wherever he wishes!"

Mr. Keller wrote to Mr. Anagnos right away. The principal said that he could help Helen. He soon found a teacher who would come live with the Kellers in Alabama. Her name was Anne Sullivan.

As a young adult, Helen learned to appreciate all types of learning. She could "listen" to music by feeling the vibrations of a piano (top). She studied her lessons by using the special alphabet for the blind called Braille (bottom).

Living, Learning, and Growing

Anne Sullivan stayed with Helen for the rest of her life. She helped teach Helen many new things. She taught her how to read and write Braille (brayl). This was a special writing for blind people. Each letter is made of dots. Anne also taught Helen subjects like **geography** (jee-AH-gruh-fee), science, and math.

After Anne taught Helen everything she knew, the two went to school together. Anne would tell Helen what the teachers were saying by moving her fingers in Helen's hand.

Helen dreamed of going to college. She worked hard and was accepted into Radcliffe, a

The Braille Alphabet

Braille is a special alphabet made up of tiny raised dots. The dots are formed in specific patterns to represent different letters of the alphabet.

a b c d e f g h i j k l m

n o p q r s t u v w x y z

NUMBERS

0 1 2 3 4 5 6 7 8 9   Literary Code

0 1 2 3 4 5 6 7 8 9   Nemeth Code

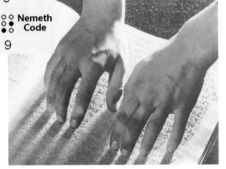

People reading the alphabet do so by feeling the dots with their hands. This alphabet was developed by a blind Frenchman named Louis Braille in 1821.

college near Harvard University in Massachusetts. It was very hard to get into this school. Helen was the first blind and deaf person ever to go there.

Anne and Helen traveled the world together. They spoke in front of large groups of people. Helen would tell Anne what she wanted to say using the finger language in Anne's hand. Then Anne would tell Helen's words to the people. Everyone admired Helen for all she had been able to accomplish.

Helen attended Radcliffe and studied languages. Many books were not available in Braille, so Anne would read them to Helen using their finger alphabet. Helen studied hard and graduated from Radcliffe with honors in 1904.

Helen was asked to write her life story. She wrote some of it using a special block letter system. The rest she typed on a typewriter. Even people who can see do not have to look at the keys when they type. Once Helen knew where the letters were on the keyboard, she could type anything she wanted very easily.

Helen communicated with others by reading lips and using the finger alphabet. In the bottom picture, she is listening to what the girl is saying.

In the picture above, she is talking to the girl by spelling her words with her hand.

Anne Sullivan (left), stayed a part of Helen's life for nearly fifty years. She continued working with Helen even after she married John Albert Macy in 1905. In her life story, Helen wrote about her teacher: "I have been frequently asked what I should do without her. I smile and answer cheerfully 'God sent her, and if He takes her, His love will fill the void.' "

Helen and Anne traveled the country performing in vaudeville shows. This picture was taken in 1920 and shows Helen getting ready for one of her performances. She's wearing a fancy dress and sits at a dressing table—without a mirror—putting on her makeup. Their performance was very popular. The pair received around $2,000 a week for performing in just two shows! They made more money than any other vaudeville performers.

Helen met with First Lady Grace Coolidge in 1926. Helen spent many years working with political leaders. She wanted to improve the conditions for physically challenged people everywhere.

Later in life, Helen performed with **vaudeville** (VAWD-vil) shows. These were variety (vuh-RY-uh-tee) shows that included dance, theater, acrobatics, performing animals, and magicians. Her family did not like this idea. They thought she would look like a clown and that people would come to laugh at her. But Helen didn't look silly, and no one laughed. People came to see an amazing person who had overcome difficult challenges. She inspired people to work hard to become their best.

Helen visits with President Calvin Coolidge. She met many presidents of the United States. When she was only seven years old, she met President Grover Cleveland. Later, on September 14, 1964, she would receive the U.S. Presidential Medal of Freedom from President Lyndon B. Johnson.

Notice the World Around You

Anne, who was much older than Helen, died in 1936. Helen missed her teacher and friend very much. However, she didn't let her death stop her from living her dreams. She continued to travel. Another friend, Polly Thomson, helped tell Helen's words to the world.

Helen helped with the American Foundation for the Blind. She helped blind soldiers after World War II. She met many presidents and leaders throughout the world. In September 1964, President Lyndon B. Johnson awarded Helen the Presidential Medal of Freedom for her life of courage and devotion to helping people with physical challenges.

Helen walks with a soldier who just lost his eyesight in battle. Behind her, Anne and Polly visit with two leaders. Helen visited injured soldiers at the Red Cross Institute for the Blind in Baltimore, Maryland.

Helen Keller passed away in her sleep on June 1, 1968. She was eighty-eight years old. She, Anne, and Polly are buried in the National Cathedral (kuh-THEE-drul) in Washington, D.C. A marker near their gravesite honors all three of them. The writing is in both English lettering and the tiny raised dots of Braille.

Helen did many things during her lifetime, but she always wished to see and hear even for just a few days. She imagined all the beautiful

Helen traveled to a school for the blind in Rome, Italy, in 1946. A friend once wrote her in a letter about this visit: "Your love inspired the children to carry on in spite of the tremendous handicaps they had to overcome. You pushed them in the direction of a more happy life."

things of the world. She dreamed of seeing the faces of her family and friends.

For those of you who can see and hear, whenever you see a beautiful flower or hear the song of a bird, think of Helen. These are things she longed to do during her lifetime but never got the chance.

CHRONOLOGY

1880	Helen Adams Keller is born in Tuscumbia, Alabama, on June 27.
1882	An illness with a high fever causes Helen to lose her sight and her hearing.
1887	Anne Sullivan arrives in Alabama to work as Helen's teacher.
1894	With Anne's help, Helen attends Wright-Humason School in New York.
1896	Helen attends Cambridge School for Young Ladies.
1900	She is the first deaf and blind person accepted to Radcliffe College.
1903	She publishes her autobiography, *The Story of My Life.*
1904	She graduates with honors from Radcliffe.
1918	Helen stars in the film *Deliverance,* which is about her life.
1919	She begins touring in vaudeville shows.
1924	She begins working with the American Foundation for the Blind.
1929	Her next book, *Midstream: My Later Life,* is published.
1934	She writes "Three Days to See."
1936	Anne Sullivan Macy dies.
1937	Helen tours Japan, with Polly Thomson as interpreter.
1955	She publishes *Teacher: Anne Sullivan Macy.*
1960	She publishes *My Religion.*
1968	Helen dies in her sleep on June 1.

TIMELINE IN HISTORY

1620	The first known book of signs for deaf people is written by Juan Pablo Bonet.
1700s	Deaf people in Martha's Vineyard, Massachusetts, develop their own system of sign language.
1788	Charles Michel De L'Eppe publishes a dictionary of sign language in France.
1817	The first American school for the deaf is founded by Thomas Hopkins Gallaudet in Hartford, Connecticut.
1821	Louis Braille develops Braille—an alphabet of raised dots.
1827	First book in Braille is published.

1856	Amos Kendall starts the Columbia Institute. This college eventually becomes Gallaudet University, a school for the deaf.
1861	Civil War begins and lasts until 1865.
1864	Abraham Lincoln signs a charter that establishes the first college for the deaf.
1870	Vaudeville becomes a popular form of entertainment in the United States.
1876	Bell invents his "electrical speech machine," now known as the telephone.
1901	William Hoy becomes first deaf baseball player in the American League.
1914	World War I begins. It lasts until 1917.
1927	Dorothy Harrison Eustis introduces to America the idea of using dogs as guides for the blind.
1930s	Electronic hearing aids are developed.
1939	World War II begins. It lasts until 1947.
1964	Robert Weitbrecht, a deaf inventor, invents the teletypewriter. A study decides that manual communication and education are superior to oral methods for the deaf.
1975	United States law is passed that requires a free public education for all children.
1980	Closed Captioning is developed.
1987	Marlee Matlin becomes first deaf actress to win an Academy Award.
1990	Americans with Disabilities Act is passed.
1991	First Lasik procedure to correct vision is performed in the United States.
1993	FCC requires that all televisions have the decoding chip for Closed Captioning.
1995	Heather Whitestone becomes the first deaf Miss America.
2001	Michael Hingson's guide dog, Roselle, helps lead him to safety from his 78th-floor office in the World Trade Center.
2007	Michigan's legislature passes a law requiring businesses, schools, and other institutions to hire interpreters for the deaf-blind.

FIND OUT MORE

Books

Adler, David A. *Helen Keller.* New York: Holiday House, 2003.

Garrett, Leslie. *Helen Keller.* London: Dorling Kindersley Publishers, Ltd., 2005.

Lawlor, Laurie. *Helen Keller: Rebellious Spirit.* New York: Holiday House, 2001.

Shichtman, Sandra H. *Helen Keller: Out of a Dark and Silent World.* Brookfield, Connecticut: Millbrook Press, 2002.

Sutcliffe, Jane. *Helen Keller.* Minneapolis: Carolrhoda Books, 2002.

Thompson, Gare. *Who Was Helen Keller?* New York: Grosset & Dunlap, 2003.

Works Consulted

Herrmann, Dorothy. *Helen Keller: A Life.* New York: A. Knopf, 1998.

Johnson, Ann Donegan. *The Value of Determination: The Story of Helen Keller.* Jolla, California: Value Communications, 1976.

Keller, Helen. *Helen Keller's Journal.* Garden City, New York: Doubleday, Doran & Company, Inc., 1938.

———. *The Story of My Life.* New York: Doubleday and Company, 1955.

———. *Teacher: Anne Sullivan Macy.* New York: Doubleday and Company, Inc., 1956.

———. "Three Days to See." Ogden, Utah: Utah School for the Deaf, 1934.

GLOSSARY

communicating (kuh-MYOO-nih-kay-ting)—Exchanging thoughts, ideas, or information or expressing feelings.

Confederate (kun-FEH-der-et)—On the side of the southern states that left the Union during the Civil War.

deaf (DEF)—Unable to hear.

frustrated (FRUS-tray-ted)—Disappointed, puzzled, or confused.

geography (jee-AH-gruh-fee)—The science of Earth's surface and everything on it.

gestures (JES-churs)—Actions or movements meant to show feelings.

vaudeville (VAWD-vil)—A type of stage performance that was very popular during the early 1900s.

vibrations (vy-BRAY-shuns)—Shaking or quivering movements.

INDEX